Recipes *for* Disaster*s*

Recipes *for* Disaster*s*

How to turn kitchen cock-ups into magnificent meals

Roni Jay

Editor: Richard Craze
Illustrator: Chris Mutter

white LaDdEr PrEss

new tricks for old dogs

Published by White Ladder Press Ltd
Great Ambrook, Near Ipplepen, Devon TQ12 5UL
01803 813343
www.whiteladderpress.com

First published in Great Britain in 2004

ISBN 0 9543914 5 4

British Library Cataloguing in Publication Data
A CIP record for this book can be obtained from the British Library.

Designed and typeset by Julie Martin Ltd
Cover design by Julie Martin Ltd
Illustrations by Chris Mutter
Printed and bound by TJ International Ltd, Padstow, Cornwall

White Ladder Press
Great Ambrook, Near Ipplepen, Devon TQ12 5UL
01803 813343
www.whiteladderpress.com

For Tony, who had the original idea for this book over 20 years ago (and gave me my love of good food), and for Yill, who revived the suggestion (and demonstrated how to cook magnificent meals).

Contents

PART 2

Notorious problem foods and how to put them right

PART 3

Things you should know before you turn the oven on

Acknowledgements

I have been lucky enough to have been helped by many better qualified people than myself in writing this book. I'd like to thank my parents Tony and Jill, Rich, Steph Croce and Guy Sheridan in particular for their help.

I'm also extremely grateful to the professional chef/restaurateurs who were kind enough to read through the manuscript for me and suggest changes and additions. All of these people run restaurants which are a delight to eat in. I can thoroughly recommend them all (as do the *Good Food Guide* and many others). Please help me express my gratitude to them by eating in their establishments next time you're in the West Country; you won't regret it. So thanks to:

Emma and Tim Ford at Little Barwick House

This is one of the most comfortable restaurants you'll find anywhere. Little Barwick House is an English country house with log fires and squishy sofas to welcome you even before you've seen the menu. The food is delicious, using many local ingredients, and the award-winning wine list is exceptional. What's more, they have rooms too (they describe themselves as a 'restaurant with rooms', demonstrating an admirable sense of priorities), so if you anticipate a thoroughly indulgent evening you don't even have to get home afterwards.

Little Barwick House, Barwick Village, Near Yeovil,
Somerset BA22 9TD   01935 423902
www.littlebarwickhouse.co.uk

Adrian and Julie Oliver at Margot's Bistro in Padstow

Our very favourite place to eat when we're on holiday in Cornwall; don't imagine there's only one top class chef in Padstow. Margot's bistro has a great atmosphere, implausibly friendly service, and terrific food. It's a gem of a place, with the added advantage that it feels like your own secret discovery, being less famous than Rick Stein's neighbouring restaurants. Check out the loo – the walls are papered with countless menus which make mouth-watering reading.

Margot's Bistro, 11 Duke Street, Padstow, Cornwall PL28 8AB
01841 533441   www.margots.co.uk

Arthur Watson and his team at the Riverside Restaurant

This well known and award-winning restaurant deserves its reputation. It's close to the harbour at West Bay and surrounded by water, so it's no surprise that it specialises in seafood, although it will serve you meat or vegetarian meals if you're daft enough to forego the most perfect fresh fish, cooked simply to preserve the taste. The atmosphere is informal and unhurried, and the desserts are delicious.

Riverside Restaurant, West Bay, Bridport, Dorset DT6 4EZ
01308 422011

Jenny Priest and Philip Silvester at Wills

Wills has a restaurant upstairs and a bistro downstairs, both of which have a relaxed atmosphere and excellent food. The menu has a wide mix of dishes which suit both of us (not easy since

we have different tastes), and they are very flexible about catering for special diets or just plain pickiness (as my husband Rich
can tell you). The service is exceptional and the staff friendly
and welcoming.

Wills, 2/3 The Plains, Totnes, Devon TQ9 5DR
08000 563006   www.eiaddio.com

Introduction

We've all been there. You're about to serve up a wonderful meal that you're really proud of, and disaster strikes. You realise that you put in Madras curry powder instead of Korma, or you remember as you're checking the roast that one of your guests is vegetarian, or you discover that the children have eaten most of the strawberries you were going to serve for dessert, or the sauce curdles at the last minute, or the fish is poached to perfection... only you haven't put the vegetables on yet.

Recipes for Disasters is designed to prevent this kind of drama from feeling like a crisis. There are few catastrophes that can't be successfully put right if you know how, and reduced to a mere hiccup that you barely notice. It's largely a matter of attitude, really, but you also need some inside knowledge of the kind of techniques professional chefs have learned over the years.

These days, few of us find ourselves worried sick because the boss is coming to dinner. If we're cooking for the boss at all it will be because they happen to be a good mate. Dinner parties aren't the stilted, nerve-wracking affairs they once were. The scariest people most of us cook for are generally the in-laws (OK, that can be pretty scary). But although we mostly cook for good friends, this doesn't mean we don't care how the meal turns out. And quite right too: who deserves a magnificent meal more than our close family and dearest friends?

The fact is that we care about our cooking as much now as ever. Our friends may be very forgiving, but we don't want to give them cause to forgive us. Frankly, we want to impress them, especially if they cooked a great meal for us last time we were over at their place. That's why we get upset when the pastry won't rise or the dessert just refuses to defrost in time.

And how do I know this? Because I've been there, plenty of times. I trained as a chef over 20 years ago, and it gave me the enthusiasm to experiment with cooking, and the urge to serve up moderately adventurous meals. However, I didn't complete the intensive four year course so my training wasn't sufficient to ensure perfection every time. Not all my meals turned out exactly as I planned. In fact, some of them were utter failures.

What the course did teach me, however, was the confidence to play around with food, and I discovered that with the right attitude and flexibility, I could serve up a damn good meal every time, even if it wasn't always the damn good meal I had planned to serve.

As well as the specific tips and advice in this book, there are a few broad guidelines to follow which will help culinary catastrophes become a thing of the past. So here are the golden rules of running a disaster-free kitchen.

Keep your guests away from the kitchen

I realise you can't redesign your house, but the problem with big family kitchens which you also eat in is that your guests can see exactly what's going on. While they sit round the table chatting, out of the corner of their eyes they can see you hopping around in hand-to-hand combat with a pudding mould that refuses to release its occupant, or secretly trying to open a tin of soup to use as an emergency sauce because the fresh one wasn't as fresh as you'd hoped and has been consigned to the bin.

Once the meal is underway, and all potential disasters are past, you can invite the guests into the kitchen, of course. Indeed, if you're well ahead and confident of the meal this time, start the evening off in the kitchen. But if there is any intimation of trouble looming, usher them from the front door straight into the living room (obviously it's a big plus here if you have a partner or a friend in the know to look after them). Then you're free to get up to all sorts of subversive salvage work in the kitchen without getting caught.

Do everything you can ahead of time

The more you can do before your guests arrive, the less chance there is for real disaster. If things go wrong you have time to rethink them or even remake them. This isn't always easy, especially on weekdays if you work full time, but you can cook some things the evening before and others at least an hour or two in advance.

Adopt a spirit of adventure

Your attitude is a big factor in a successful salvage operation. The more relaxed, flexible and creative you are in an emergency, the better you will cope and the more you will enjoy it. This book is intended to help you view kitchen crises as a challenge, and enjoy finding ways to overcome them. Some of us are better equipped for this psychologically than others, of course, but we can all learn.

For me, the biggest lesson was to be flexible. If the puff pastry on top of the steak and kidney pie didn't rise, I used to get really upset. Now I just whip the unco-operative pastry off and serve steak and kidney casserole instead. Once you realise that the meal you end up with doesn't have to be the meal you first thought of, it's tremendously liberating.

If you don't tell 'em, they won't know

It doesn't occur to your guests that everything has gone wrong unless you make it obvious. If you apologise as you serve up the dish and tell them what just happened, of course they'll know. But if you serve them steak and kidney casserole without any mention of the badly behaved pastry (which not only let you down but, what's worse, let itself down), why would they know?

Confidence is everything

The more outrageously you remedy your potential disasters, the more you will get away with, believe me. If you rename a dish and serve it with panache (sorry, no recipe for that), you can get away with anything. Tell your guests as you serve a baked pudding that's sunk in the middle, "This is called Norfolk Collapsy Pudding" and they'll believe you and assume it's cooked to perfection. If they happen to be from Norfolk, tell them it's called Cornish Well Cake. Have fun; it pays.

Overdose your guests on good wine and good company

Let's be honest; if they've had enough to drink, they won't notice much. A couple of extra glasses before eating (ideally champagne if you can run to it; on an empty stomach it gets them merry faster than anything), and they'll appreciate good food without studying it too closely. For those who are driving and not drinking, the company of good friends – especially friends knocking back champagne – will soon put them in a similar spirit. If you start sulking or getting upset about the meal you can bring everyone down. In fact, the real disaster is not the crisis in the kitchen but your anxiety about it, which can ruin everyone's evening. But with confidence and flexibility, and a cheerful enthusiasm for a challenge, you'll soon infuse everyone with the kind of animated enjoyment that makes them blind to any imperfections in the kitchen department.

There are few kitchen cock-ups that can't be successfully salvaged if you know how. With a bit of calm and clear thinking, and a modest but well thought-out store cupboard, all it takes is a willingness to adapt and a bit of know-how. Who knows? You could even end up inventing a new classic dish to add to your repertoire. So pour yourself a glass of wine, relax, and add the following recipes for disasters to your kitchen scrapbook.

Dinner party excuses no.18

Concealing total disaster

"I was trying to create the authentic Chinese takeaway taste – I do hope I've succeeded."

Part 1

Classic disasters *and* how to remedy them

It won't turn ʇno

I made this beautiful vegetable terrine as a starter. But when I came to turn it out it was stuck firmly in the mould and wouldn't budge. I was so upset I chucked it all in the bin and gave everyone crisps and dips instead.

Struggling from Stockton

How frustrating. I hate that thing of prancing round the kitchen trying every possible angle of attack on some stubborn dish that refuses to release its grip. I've ended up with a kitchen sink full of rejected tools, from sharp knives and long-handled spoons to pliers and hammers. As a general rule, if you want to cook anything that has to turn out, it's best to do it well in advance just in case there are problems. In the worst case scenario you then have time to start again. If you haven't got time to begin again from scratch, it might be better to avoid this kind of dish unless you're really confident and have made it before.

Having said that, some dishes that need turning out are always more promising than others. For example, sponge puddings rarely get completely stuck even though they may need a little encouragement with a palette knife. And anything you can melt such as ice cream or gelatine based terrines and puddings should be salvageable.

Generally speaking, it's worth making sure you don't overcook these kinds of dishes because that always makes it harder to turn them out. Keep a watchful eye and whip them out of the oven as soon as they're done.

THINKING AHEAD

The professional chefs' technique for getting things to turn out is to line the container with clingfilm. Believe it or not it won't melt, and you can lift the whole thing out easily and peel off the clingfilm. (And you thought they relied on talent to turn out perfect looking meals.)

Before you start fretting, consider whether the mould you're using is presentable enough to serve the food in without turning it out. Failing that, here are the best methods for getting recalcitrant dishes out of their containers:

- If the dish is capable of melting – or even just relaxing under the influence of heat – run a bowl or sink of hot water and dip the mould into it up to the level where the contents are sticking. Test it frequently to see if it will turn out; you don't want to leave your ice cream mould in the water for five minutes only to find you've melted all the ice cream (in which case see the next section 'It won't set'). This works for jellies and anything gelatine-based too.

- Use a palette knife to ease the thing out of the dish. It may help – depending on the dish in question – to heat the palette knife in a mug of boiling water or to dip it in oil first. If you don't have a palette knife you can get by with any blunt, round-ended knife, but do go out and buy a short palette knife when you get the chance. Even cooks who never have any cock-ups in the kitchen (not that I've ever met any of them) find it a useful piece of equipment.

- If Mohammed won't go to the mountain… Let's be lateral here. The object of the exercise is to separate the dish from the container. Sometimes it's possible to switch your focus to the container. You don't want to take a hammer to china and leave wicked shards in the food for your guests to eat. And you probably don't want to destroy granny's favourite pudding mould which has been in the family for generations. But if your mould is made of tupperware or plastic or thin metal you might make a policy decision to ruin the mould in order to save the dish. This has the added advantage that it makes it easier to blame the whole problem on the mould. You have to find someone or something other than yourself to blame, and a completely trashed mould can't argue back.

- Sometimes you just can't get the thing out without making a bit of a mess of it. So make a mess of it. Keep it to a minimum, of course, and then disguise it afterwards. A few strategically placed sprigs of mint, or a dollop of clotted cream (which you had previously planned to serve separately perhaps) can cover up a mulitude of injuries. You can dust sweet dishes with cocoa powder or icing sugar sprinkled through a sieve.

- You may be able to slice or cut up the dish into separate portions and serve each on its own plate. Give the untidiest ones to the family and give the perfect ones to the guests. And disguise them all with a garnish too if that helps, of course.

> **SALVAGE SECRETS**
>
> Just about any slightly soiled dish will look better for a touch of garnishing; it draws the eye away from the damage and can sometimes obscure it entirely. You don't have

to use the naff sprig of parsley and a twist of lemon thing. You can garnish with anything. Herbs work well for savoury dishes, cream is a good standby, fresh flowers look great on puddings (make sure you warn your guests if they're not actually edible). Slices of fruit or salad vegetables, chopped nuts, chocolate flakes... the list is as expansive as your imagination.

Dinner party excuses no.21

It won't turn out

"We're into saving the planet so we don't create unnecessary washing up."

It won't set

I made a rhubarb mousse in the morning so it would have plenty of time to set, but as the day wore on it was still runny. By the end of the afternoon it was clear it wasn't going to set so I just had to serve it up all runny. I was so embarrassed.

Red-faced from Royston

As with all these dishes that are supposed to do something (such as set) after you've made them, it's always best to give yourself time for emergency treatment if things don't go right. But even at the last minute, a bit of confidence and a certain amount of front will get you through. There are broadly speaking two ways to deal with this disaster, although time may narrow your choice down to one.

Try again

If you have time, you can tip the whole thing out and have another bash. It's particularly helpful if you have an inkling as to *why* the damn thing didn't set; it will give you a clue as to how to remedy the problem. Maybe you recall having a sort of feeling at the time that the fruit purée was a bit runny, for example. In that case, pour off a bit of the liquid before you try again.

Dinner party excuses no.8

It won't set

"It's a new recipe – raspberry jelly soup."

The best ways to get something to set are to add gelatine (which it's always worth keeping in your kitchen first aid store), or to fold in something stiff such as whipped cream or egg whites. You might even be able to use an inventive solution such as broken amaretto biscuits.

Another option, if it suits the dish, is to fold in some beaten egg white and then cook the thing in pastry cases to create mini quiches or tarts.

Repackage the dish

So what if you haven't got time to try again? This is where the confidence comes in. You need to serve the dish up runny (what choice do you have?) but present it as a different dish which *is supposed to be runny*. For example, for rhubarb fool which won't thicken up, add crushed meringue and tell your guests it's Rhubarb Eton Mess.

Here's another idea. Sweet soups are quite fashionable. So you can pour a very runny mousse into a tureen – maybe even thin it down a bit more (go on, enjoy it) – and serve it in bowls with a ladle. Garnish the top with a swirl of cream and a sprinkle of flaked almonds or something. Your guests might think you're suddenly getting very trendy or far more interesting than usual – either of which is good – but it would never cross their minds you were simply covering up your mistakes.

If sweet soup isn't an option with this dish, invent something else which is. For example a smoked salmon terrine that hasn't set could make a very tasty sauce to pour over hard-boiled eggs as a novel take on egg mayonnaise. Now come on, if someone served that up to you, you wouldn't think 'Oh, I get it. The terrine wouldn't set', would you? You'd think, 'How interesting, I've never had this before. I never knew Terry was such an original cook.'

It won't rise

I made what I thought was a wonderful steamed pudding when we had friends over for Sunday lunch. But when I turned it out, it hadn't risen at all.

Flattened from Fishbourne

Well, look on the bright side – at least you managed to turn it out without trouble. Seriously, things not rising isn't nearly as bad as you think. It's all a matter of perception. *You* know it was supposed to rise, so you're disappointed. But your guests only know it was meant to rise if you tell them so. If you serve it up and announce, "This is called Sussex flat cake. It's an unusual regional recipe I discovered recently," it will never dawn on them that it's actually an unrisen steamed pudding.

You can add to the effect by prettying the thing up in some way. Sprinkle it with chopped hazelnuts or add a dollop of ice cream and it will be even less reminiscent of a steamed pudding. Or cut it into thin slices (usually quite easy with things that are supposed to rise and haven't) and serve them neatly arranged on a plate.

This works for far more than steamed puddings, of course. For example, cakes that don't rise can be reinvented as soft biscuits, and countless puddings can be re-dressed and renamed to fool even the most educated palate. It's a good rule to serve whipped cream with heavy puddings to lighten them. Do this with your unrisen pudding and it consolidates the impression that it was always intended to be rich and heavy.

THINKING AHEAD

If you're concerned about a particular recipe which is supposed to rise and you suspect may not, cook a small sample in advance if you can just to check that it's going to work.

Yorkshire pudding

I'm not bothering to give any help to people who try to impress with soufflés when they don't know what they're doing. If you can serve up a mean soufflé you don't need any help from me. If you can't, practise in private until you're sure of yourself. If you choose to embarrass yourself in front of guests before you know what you're doing, you have only yourself to blame for the results.

But Yorkshire pudding is a different matter. You are entitled to expect this down-to-earth, traditional dish to work for you. In fact, however, it is a common problem in the 'will it or won't it' rise category. Unrisen Yorkshire pudding is fine, just stodgier than the risen version. And if you don't like stodge, why have Yorkshire pudding anyway? Some people even prefer it that way. Just make it clear that you're one of them, and you've deliberately made it this way. Call them Yorkshire biscuits.

For what to do about puff pastry that doesn't rise, see page 81.

It's burnt

All I did was answer the phone! When I got back, the chicken pieces I'd been frying before putting them in the casserole were burnt.

Frazzled from Frimley

How you deal with this all depends on what you mean by burnt. Some things are supposed to be burnt, like crème brûlée, or the skin on a traditional rice pudding (at least in my opinion).

There's a temptation, if you're the emotional type, to burst into tears and throw the whole lot in the bin. But actually, you'll usually find that a lot of it is salvageable if you take a more objective view of it. You may only need to discard one or two pieces of chicken, or the edges of a cake. Here are some thoughts which might spark off some salvage ideas for your own predicament:

- If you have to discard only some of the food, such as the curry that was at the bottom of the pan and got the brunt of the heat, you can use the rest and bulk the meal out with extra rice (or whatever suits the dish in question).

- If your chicken pieces are not so much burnt as overbrowned, you could adapt the dish to include more robust flavours which will cover the taste. For example, you might caremelise some onions (just cook them long and slow in a frying pan with some oil) and add them.

- If you burn the pastry on your apple pie, you can always remove the pastry and serve the stewed apple on its own (you can vary this approach with all sorts of pies, both sweet and savoury). You can add whipped cream – either as a topping, or folded in to make a fool, if you have time to cool the apple down. Or quickly rustle up a crumble topping to replace the pastry, or top with ratafia biscuits, or whisked egg whites with sugar (stick it back in the oven for a few minutes to brown)... you get the idea.

- If the edges of a cake you're baking for tea get burnt, cut them off and ice the cake to conceal your handiwork.

- If you burn any fairly hard food, such as crusty bread, you can use a grater to scrape off the burnt tops or edges.

THINKING AHEAD

Always **take the pan off the heat when you go to answer the phone or the door, or to sort out the children's squabbles. It's easy to be optimistic and think it will be quick, but it's not worth the risk. After all, you've nothing to lose.**

If the food really is burnt to a charcoal-crisp texture that crumbles to dust when you touch it, even I would concede that there's very little you can do except bin it. Your options then are something like this:

- This is where emergency standbys in the freezer can be so helpful (see page 106) for last minute replacements.

- If you're lucky, of course, you may have the time and the ingredients to start again.

- If the thing that got burnt wasn't essential, you could just leave it out. For example, you don't *have* to serve Yorkshire puddings with your roast beef, or onion bhajis with your curry.

Dinner party excuses no.56

It's burnt

"You've heard of film noir? Well, this is crême brulée noir."

It's collapsed

The salmon mousse I made was looking great until I turned it out of the mould. Then it just collapsed. I was so upset; I was cooking for new friends and I'd really wanted the meal to look good.

Depressed from Darlington

There's no point crying over spilt milk, nor over a collapsed mousse. Look, once it's collapsed, it's collapsed and there's nothing you can do to put it back together. You have two options, depending on the extent of the disaster.

Partial collapse

Maybe you're exaggerating because you're upset. Perhaps the thing isn't so much collapsed as simply crumbling a bit round the edges. In that case the solution is simple: hide the damage. You can decorate the edges of a salmon mousse with slices of cucumber strategically positioned to conceal its imperfections. A cake or pudding can have whipped cream piped on it. If piping is beyond you (and I quite understand if it is) you could add slices of fruit or pour chocolate sauce over the whole thing.

Total collapse

Right. Take a deep breath. Chill. Rethink. You are not going to be serving up the meal you first thought of. You're going to be serving up a different – but equally good – dish. In this case, about the only thing you can do is to cut your losses and chop or mash the whole thing up.

Salmon mousse can be mashed and then spooned into individual ramekin dishes with a sprig of dill and a twist of cucumber on each one. No one but you will ever know. Or you could wrap it in a pancake and maybe pour a light sauce over the top before you serve it. Jelly can be chopped and dished up in wine glass-

Dinner party excuses no.51

It's collapsed

"This is known as inside out pudding."

es topped with whipped cream. Chocolate mousses can be folded back together until smooth and served in a large dish sprinkled with grated chocolate.

The fact is that there's nothing wrong with the taste of your dish; it's simply a matter of presentation. So come up with another way of presenting the same food which doesn't look as if it's gone wrong.

I followed a delicious Edwardian recipe for port jelly once, for a party of about 18 guests. I set the jelly in two moulds and planned to turn the smaller, tall jelly out inside the ring mould of jelly to form a kind of tower (don't know what I was thinking of). Sadly, when I turned the smaller jelly out, it broke up. We'd already finished our main course so I didn't have much time. I chopped up the smaller jelly and spooned it into the round hole in the middle of the larger, ring jelly. Then I added a bit of whipped cream and some lemon zest. You'd never have guessed from the compliments I got for the dish that the jelly wasn't served as planned. (Actually by the time the guests had finished it they were too sozzled to notice much anyway. It was the most alcoholic thing I've ever eaten.)

It has burnt bits in it

Help! I was heating the milk and eggs to make home-made ice cream, when I noticed the mixture was full of bits. On investigation, it turned out that the saucepan hadn't been properly washed up from the scrambled egg at breakfast. So the bits were fresh and wouldn't taste, but they looked awful. I didn't have enough eggs to throw the mixture away and start again. What should I have done?

Shattered from Stockport

This can be very frustrating, particularly when you know the bits aren't in the least harmful and won't taste. You might have started with a bowl or pan that wasn't as clean as you thought, or maybe you spilt a spoonful of sesame seeds or chopped mushrooms or something into the bowl while you were preparing a different dish. Or perhaps you've overheated an egg-based sauce and tiny pieces of egg have set in it.

The answer, perhaps surprisingly, is to add more bits. Camouflage, that's what you're after. Take the ice cream: if you add a bit of almond essence and some chopped nuts, the ice cream will be delicious and the renegade bits will go unnoticed. The assumption will be that they are chopped nuts. If you don't like nuts, try adding pieces of honeycomb (if you can find a

Crunchie bar to chop up) or some brown breadcrumbs to make brown bread ice cream (it's delicious).

If the bits that have infiltrated your recipe are large enough, you can pick them out quite easily. If they're not big enough for that but are still too large, you may be able to put the whole thing through a fine sieve successfully, or in the blender to break them up. For example, if you've spilt cornflakes in the casserole, you could remove the meat (and rinse it off if necessary), then bizz up the sauce before you replace it. The casserole will have a different consistency, of course, but it will taste just as good.

Dinner party excuses no.11

It has bits in it

"It's an old recipe of my grandmother's. It's called speckled syllabub."

SALVAGE SECRETS

Professional chefs always have stick blenders in the kitchen (you know, those hand-held blender/choppers you put into the mixture). These are great for smoothing out overcooked ice cream in which the egg white has started to set into very small lumps.

It's curdled

I was serving apple pie with home-made custard. I've made custard before and it's been fine. But this time it took it upon itself to curdle. I was so frustrated, and it was an important part of the dish. What should I have done?

Pissed off from Paignton

Curdling is one of those painful things which always happens just when everything was going so well. Suddenly the carefully bound or emulsified ingredients separate, and you can't seem to get them to recombine. How you deal with it depends on what has curdled.

Sauces

A sauce such as custard curdles when you heat it because the eggs start to cook too much and form hard lumps in the sauce. You can't uncook the eggs, but you can simply pass the whole thing through a fine sieve to take out the lumps. This works for just about all sauces. Often, simply putting the sauce through the blender will take the lumps out.

Cakes and sponges

When you add the eggs to the creamed butter and sugar, they're supposed to combine into one smooth mixture. But sometimes they form a curdled assembly of tiny lumps floating in beaten egg. Don't worry about it. Simply keep going, add the flour, and by the time the whole thing is mixed and cooked you won't be able to tell the difference.

To find out how to salvage curdled mayonnaise and hollandaise see page 89.

Dinner party excuses no.16

It's curdled

"It's a traditional Yugoslavian sauce – Split mayonnaise."

It won't defrost

We had some work colleagues coming to dinner and I'd stuffed a joint of pork in advance and frozen it. I took it out of the freezer at lunchtime but, when it was time to cook it, it still hadn't defrosted.

Bitter from Birmingham

What is it with defrosting? The time it takes is completely unpredictable. You can defrost half a dozen chicken wings in an hour one day, and the next week it takes you all morning. If you get caught out, however, there are plenty of things you can do. Some of these should be obvious, but even the obvious is worth reiterating when you're panicking.

Cook the damn thing anyway

The fastest way to defrost your stuffed pork is to stick it in the oven. So you can always just go ahead and cook it. It may be slightly tougher, but frankly your guests probably won't notice. However, you do need to be sure that it's cooked thoroughly right through to avoid giving your guests food poisoning (which is worse than a duff meal, to be honest). The outside of the pork may be ruined this way, so be prepared to make a sauce to pour over it to obscure this.

Eat later

This should require no further explanation.

Put it under running water

Put the thing you want to defrost under running cold water, in a waterproof container or a plastic bag. This will speed up the defrosting process.

THINKING AHEAD

If you freeze something liquid or slushy, such as a sauce, in a plastic bag you can't get it out until it has defrosted. The wrinkles of the bag are all squished into the contents and can't be peeled away. If you freeze the thing in a rigid plastic container, however, you can loosen the edges by submerging the thing in hot water, and then you can tip out the whole lump easily. The point of this is that you can then easily defrost your sauce by heating it up in a saucepan.

Use a microwave

The simplest method of defrosting. If you're reading this section you probably haven't got one, of course. But that doesn't mean that your neighbours haven't. Ask someone nearby if you can borrow theirs. Be aware that a microwave won't necessarily be able to defrost right through to the centre of a large frozen object. You may need to let the rest defrost naturally or cut the thing up into smaller pieces.

Dinner party excuses no.44

It won't defrost

"Boeuf Wellington ice cream, anyone?"

Cut it up

This might not be ideal with your joint of pork. But a lot of things can be sawn up or cut with a sharp knife while still frozen. The smaller pieces defrost much quicker.

Pass it off as a frozen dish

If the dish you're trying to defrost is not intended to be cooked your options for defrosting are limited. Maybe you froze individual desserts and you can't microwave or heat them up without cooking them. If the airing cupboard doesn't do the trick in time, you may have to claim the pudding is supposed to be frozen. Just describe it as a parfait instead of a mousse, for example (a parfait is a frozen mousse so you're quite within your rights to do this).

SALVAGE SECRETS

For reasons which are not scientifically clear to me, you will find that putting the food in front of a cold electric fan will also speed up the defrosting process. Another handy tip (more obviously plausible this time) is to stand the thing on a metal tray as this conducts heat better than wood or plastic.

It's difficult to defrost things too soon. After all, so long as they're in a fridge, most things will happily last a couple of days at least after defrosting. So get into the habit of taking things out of the freezer the day before you want to use them and defrosting them in the fridge.

It's dried out

I put some stuffed lamb medallions in the oven for half an hour, and when I took them out to serve them they were really dry. There was nothing I could do, so I just had to dish them up as they were.

Dusty from Dawlish

If you have a range cooker this problem will make you feel very smug, since almost nothing ever dries out in a range. If you haven't got a range cooker, however, you'll be sympathetic to a common problem. There are two basic solutions to this, one cheaper than the other.

The expensive solution is to go out and buy a range cooker and, if necessary, a new kitchen to fit it into. The cheap solution is to disguise the dryness with something wet: a sauce.

What do you think gravy is for? Most roast dinners would be pretty dry without it. You just need to cook up a quick sauce of some kind to counteract the dryness.

● You can serve mayonnaise with poached salmon (and you don't even have to make it yourself).

- You can make a gravy using the pan juices.

- You can boil double cream in a pan or roasting dish until it has reduced to the consistency of a sauce. Add anything you like to give additional flavour – spices, wine, chopped fruit or nuts, chopped herbs, whatever will set off the flavour of the dried out dish you're serving it with.

- You can just serve cream with any dessert (never invite people round for a meal without having a spare pot of cream in the fridge – see 'Essential store cupboard first aid', page 103).

Dinner party excuses no.31

It's dried out

"Who's for poached salmon crunch?"

SALVAGE SECRETS

If you serve cream as an emergency accompaniment for any reason, always serve it whipped. It looks far more intentional. A couple of drops of vanilla essence and some icing sugar will turn it into chantilly cream, which is even more convincing.

You've put in too much of one ingredient

I was just adding a bit of red food colouring to the strawberry fool when my hand must have slipped and I accidentally poured in half a bottle. My strawberry fool turned a violent shade of puce.

Scarlett from Shetland

I don't like to criticise, but you've made a classic mistake here (I know because I've done it myself). Still, once it's done that advice isn't much help, so here are some more useful suggestions.

- **Scoop it back out before it's too late.** Before you panic, are you sure you can't salvage the disaster? Often you have time to spoon the worst of the excess out of the bowl or pan. This usually works with the excess of food colouring if you're fairly quick.

- **Boil off extra liquid.** If it's liquid you've added too much of you may be able to reduce it down by boiling until the water evaporates. Too runny a casserole, for example, or a watery soup can be remedied like this.

- **Thicken it up.** If you've made your fruit purée too runny, for example, you can often add a little gelatine (following the instructions on the packet) to thicken it. You can thicken a runny sauce which you've added too much liquid to by making a roux of melted butter and flour and adding the sauce to it gradually (to prevent lumps) in order to thicken it. If you have a tin of beans, add the syrup from it to savoury dishes to thicken the sauce.

●● **Bulk it out.** If you've doubled up on one ingredient accidentally, just double the quantities of everything else. You'll end up with too much, of course, but you can freeze half of it. If you've run out of some key ingredients you may be able to substitute others. For example, bulk out an oversalted stew with extra vegetables if you don't have any more meat. Or add extra whipped cream to the very pink strawberry fool to dilute the colour.

● *Change the recipe.* As with so many potential disasters, you can change the nature of the dish. So a parsnip soup which was supposed to have a tiny pinch of cumin in it until your hand slipped becomes a cumin and parsnip soup.

THINKING AHEAD

If you have an ingredient you really don't want to add too much of, never pour it straight into the bowl or pan. Always measure out the amount you need into a spoon or bowl first so you can't overdo it.

There are some specific ingredients which you may be able to counter the effects of with an antidote. However, there is a limit to how much excess they can deactivate so don't rely on them too heavily.

● *Curry powder* can be reduced in strength by adding honey or sugar.

- *Salt* can be reduced by adding peeled and quartered potatoes. After a few minutes cooking you remove the potatoes which should have absorbed the excess salt. Some people swear by this trick, others insist it has no effect whatever. I figure if you've got a casserole with too much salt in it, it can't hurt to try it.

- *Grease* in stews can be removed by throwing in a few ice cubes. Before they melt the fat will stick to them and you can take them out.

On the subject of stews, they actually taste better on the second day. If you cook them ahead you can chill them and then just lift out the fat.

Dinner party excuses no.21

You've put in too much of one ingredient

"This is a traditional dish in Salt Lake City."

A key ingredient is mi ing

I was cooking a recipe for chicken pieces coated in a delicious buttery, herby sauce. I went out into the garden to pick some fresh herbs for it and when I got back, the cat had stolen four of the six chicken pieces off the work surface. I can't stretch two chicken quarters to feed six people. Bloody cat!

Livid from Liverpool

I'd be tempted to eat the cat (only joking – don't write in). You don't have to have a cat, of course, to encounter this problem. Children make good cat substitutes here and find it easier to open fridge and cupboard doors, too. But even with well trained children or none at all, you're still not safe. Your key ingredient could have gone bad, or you might have assumed you had plenty of flour in the store cupboard only to find that actually you have almost none.

In the worst case scenario, of course, you may have to fall back on your store cupboard to whip up a completely new meal in moments (see page 103), or use a meal from the freezer (see page 106). But it's surprising how rarely you need to resort to this if you just use a bit of smart thinking.

Don't throw out the baby with the bath water

Take those chicken quarters, for instance. There's no need at all to waste the fabulous herby, buttery sauce. Simply cook up some pasta and use it on that instead. What's more, you can cook and break up the chicken you've still got and add it to the sauce.

If you're making a provençale sauce and you find that all the tomatoes have gone bad, just replace them with extra peppers and courgettes, for example, and don't call it a provençale. If the potatoes to go with the meat have gone green, cook rice instead.

A KEY INGREDIENT IS MISSING

Fruit is another ingredient that can let you down. When it's time to make the apple pie, all the apples are mouldy. Never mind, maybe you could make a banana crumble instead (add some lemon zest to take off the sweetness and it's delicious).

Or maybe it's the crumble that's the problem. No flour? How about a crème brulée topping for your fruit instead? Or make a rice pudding to go with the poached or stewed fruit.

If you forgot to buy the chocolate for the chocolate cheesecake, make a sultana cheesecake instead. If there's no ice cream left to go with the dessert, make a real custard instead, or make chantilly cream: whip up some cream with a drop of vanilla essence and a pinch of icing sugar.

SALVAGE SECRETS

If you think your revised dessert doesn't look as sophisticated as you'd hoped, just serve it in individual dishes instead of out of one big dish. It always looks fancier.

You've dropped

It was that cat again! Our guests were already sitting down at the dining table. I had taken the roast pheasant out of the oven and was just transferring it to the meat dish using the carving fork when the wretched creature scampered under my feet. I tripped, and the pheasant flew off the end of the fork and landed among three years accumulated dust and fluff behind the fridge.

Livid from Liverpool

Even dropping food isn't usually as terminal as it seems. The only time you really will have to abandon the dish and start again is if broken shards of china or glass are mixed in with the food. If this happens, start again or use a quick standby or freezer meal (see page 106).

In the case of the pheasant, clearly you have to dig it out from behind the fridge and wash it thoroughly. Use hot water so as not to cool it down too much. Then put it back in the oven for five minutes to dry off a bit and recrisp, and kill off any dodgy bacteria that had taken up residence behind the fridge. Yes, I know the vegetables will get cold but you can put them back in the oven too, and/or make sure the gravy at least is served piping hot to warm everything up on the plate.

And in future, shut that cat out of the kitchen when you're cooking.

If the dropping process has damaged the food beyond merely accumulating dust, you're into salvaging collapsed food. As you'll find on page 26 your chief options are variations on chopping it up or disguising the damage.

What you do in your own home is your business, but obviously I should point out that dropped food can pick up germs it shouldn't have come in contact with in the normal way of things. Think twice before you poison your guests. If you're really tempted to go ahead and poison them, you might question what you are doing inviting them over in the first place.

The last minute drop

Suppose you drop the food as you're carrying it to the table to serve? Not only is the food ruined but you've made a fool of yourself in front of your guests too. Don't worry; this never needs to happen. You can prevent it by following this simple rule: *never carry food to the table yourself.* Always get someone else to carry it.

If you're old, ill, or female you can ask someone young, healthy and male to carry it for you without needing to give a reason. If you are male, or the fittest person in the room, or (quite understandably) don't like playing the feeble woman card, just give yourself another job to do. For example, "Could someone just carry this to the table for me while I go and get the cream/finish the gravy/shut the cat out of the kitchen?"

This doesn't rule out the possibility that the food may get dropped, of course. But if it happens, instead of being the perpetrator you become the injured party. All that work you put into the meal and then some thoughtless bastard just comes along and drops it. You'll be the object of everyone's sympathy and you can be magnanimous in your forgiveness of the fall guy who actually dropped the thing.

Dinner party excuses no.37

You've dropped it

"It's called lemon meringue frappé."

You forgot to turn the oven ●n

We had one of my children's friends over with her parents for Sunday lunch. I didn't know the family that well and I wanted to impress them, so I decided to do a roast joint. I bought a leg of lamb, and put it in the oven. When I checked it, about half an hour before we were due to eat, I realised that I'd forgotten to turn the oven on an hour and a half before. We ended up eating lunch at 3pm, and I felt dreadfully embarrassed. What should I have done?

Humiliated from Hartlepool

Whoops. It's so easy to do in the rush of getting a meal ready. But actually, there are plenty of ways round it, once you know. For a start, why not eat at 3pm? What's wrong with that? It's simply a matter of having the confidence to carry this kind of thing off. You simply say, "We always have lunch at three in this house. Sunday mornings are such good things we like them to go on for as long as possible." It also helps if you can find something to serve as a pre-meal snack, such as a large bag of posh crisps and a dip (see page 103 for suggestions). Not only does it stave off the worst of the hunger, but it also supports the impression that the 3pm start time was intentional.

But maybe you have to eat at the planned time, or thereabouts. Perhaps half the guests have to leave by three. In that case, you need to change the menu. You'll find a basic suggestion below, but you can obviously make as many variations to it as you like, according to your tastes and what ingredients you have to hand.

The salvage operation

Now let's be logical here. The reason that the meat won't cook in time is twofold: firstly it's in too big a lump, and secondly an oven doesn't provide a sufficiently direct, high source of heat. Well, let's change that.

Begin by chopping the meat into smaller pieces. You can slice it, chop it into small strips, separate duck or chicken into leg and breast portions: you choose, according to how much time you have (less time = smaller pieces), and what kind of meat you're cooking. Some roasting cuts can be tough if you fry them, so it's generally better to cut dark meat into thin strips. OK, that's the first part solved; your meat is now small enough to cook quickly. The second problem – needing a stronger source of heat – can be solved by cooking the meat on top of the cooker in a frying pan.

Here's the creative bit now, and if you're relaxed enough it should be fun. If you're not relaxed enough, have a drink first. This isn't a proper recipe because I have no idea what ingredients you have, but I'll have a bash at the general idea:

- Put a bit of oil in your largest frying pan, and put it on the heat. Easy so far.

- You could throw the chopped meat in next but, if you have the odd onion in your kitchen, maybe you could chop that up and put it in the pan first. Likewise, bacon is an option at this stage, especially if you're cooking chicken.

- Now add the meat, and cook it through (you can always part cook larger pieces of meat in the microwave first).

- The next thing you need is some kind of liquid. This stops the meat drying out, and provides a medium to carry the extra flavours you add. It also means you can make the whole thing look like a casserole of some kind when you serve it. My favourite liquid addition at this stage is double cream. It will soak up all the flavours in the pan and, if you leave it to bubble for a few minutes, it will reduce down to a delicious thick sauce.

•• If you don't have any cream, you can add stock or a mixture of wine and stock. If you want a thick sauce, just stir in a tablespoonful of flour before you add the liquid.

● Now you're free to add any other flavourings you have around that you fancy, but you've already got a very tasty dish there on its own – extra flavourings are a bonus at this stage.

Flavours to add

I'll give you a few ideas here, just to kick you off. Once you've got the idea you'll be able to come up with all sorts of variations of your own. Obviously you can combine flavours, and you'll need to season with salt and pepper too.

● *For beef:* Onions, cream and plenty of paprika will give you a delightful variation on a classic goulash.

● *For lamb:* If you were planning to serve mint jelly, mint sauce or redcurrant jelly with the roast, put some in with the sauce instead. Go gently and taste as you go so you don't overdo it.

◖ *For pork:* You could peel and core an apple and slice it into the sauce, or add some apple sauce if you have any.

● *For chicken:* Just onions, bacon and cream is delicious with chicken. It's even better if you add blue cheese.

•• *For turkey:* Try adding a mild touch of curry powder and any spices you have around that seem to suit – maybe cumin, or cardamom.

● *For duck:* Empty a tin of cherries into the pan, or add the zest and juice of a fresh orange.

THINKING AHEAD

If you really don't want this to happen, get an Aga or a range cooker. They're on all the time, so you don't have to remember to turn them on before you cook. Aga owners are generally very smug about their cookers, but then it's more fun being smug than serving up stone cold, raw food. If you lack either the money or the space for a range cooker, console yourself with the thought that just occasionally, range cookers go out because there's no fuel left, or the wind is in the wrong direction (they can be quite capricious). And when that happens, their smug owners have to wait hours for them to heat up again.

Dinner party excuses no.75

You forgot to turn the oven on

"Did I say we'd be having roast beef? I meant steak tartare."

Vital equipment is broken

I really like home-made soup and I think it looks good to serve it at a dinner party. So I decided on a cream of vegetable soup. I cut the vegetables into large pieces to cook them so I could put it all through the blender when they were done. Only the blender decided not to work. I was left with a pot full of vegetable chunks in a thin liquid.

Switched off from Scunthorpe

If it isn't the blender it could be the electric whisk, the microwave, the kettle or even the oven. You should be able to cope without most pieces of equipment so long as you think clearly. Most kitchen gadgets are designed to make an existing job easier, rather than do a job that can't be done any other way.

When I was at catering college (many years ago) one of the few things I remember all too clearly was being made to whisk everything with a hand whisk, just so we wouldn't forget how to do it if the electric whisk broke down. This meant egg whites, cream, sauces and so on – every time. It was wrist-breaking stuff and always seemed quite pointless to me; it's not as if hand whisking is a skilled task that takes years to learn. Surely in an emergency we could have picked up a hand whisk and worked out how to use it as we went along?

It is true though that most jobs can be done at least well enough without fancy equipment. Maybe your crinkle cut sauté potatoes are straight cut if the mandolin cutter snaps in half, or your bread has to be baked in the oven because the fuse has blown on the breadmaker. But it shouldn't be impossible to improvise or adjust.

Clearly the solution to this kind of problem depends on what piece of equipment has broken. So here's a round up of some of the equipment we most commonly rely on and how to cope when it lets you down.

- *Electric whisk* A hand whisk is a pain and takes a bit longer, but it's perfectly manageable. If you're such a committed gadget freak that you don't own one, a fork will do – or two forks back to back – although you wouldn't want to do it too often.

- *Blender* A potato masher will often do instead; it will change the texture but it may well taste just as good. You could certainly mash up your vegetable soup, or push it through a sieve. Or just chop things finely with a knife.

- *Microwave* You may have to delay the meal slightly, but you can always use a conventional oven instead of a microwave.

- *Oven* You can cook oven meals on the stove top (see 'You forgot to turn the oven on' page 50) if necessary, and you can adapt stove-top meals to cook in the oven. You're only really in trouble if both oven and stove top are broken. In this case even I will concede that you'll probably have to change the menu.

- *Weighing scales* If you use electronic scales, you won't be able to weigh anything if they break down. Just remember, one ounce of flour is one rounded tablespoon, and one ounce of sugar is a flat tablespoon. I've always found that's enough to get you through.

● *Kitchen mixer* There's nothing a kitchen mixer can do that you can't do by hand instead. It's just more boring. The same goes for your garlic crusher, kitchen timer and electric juicer. Even toasters and kettles aren't essential. You can always use the grill or boil a pan of water. So long as your judgement isn't clouded by panic, the solution is generally obvious.

● *Freezer* If you live far enough north this won't matter, at least not in winter. Further south, however, you may have to regroup. Obviously food you're planning to cook can be transferred to the fridge until you're ready to cook it. It's food you want to serve frozen, such as home-made ice cream, that's the problem. Obviously the ice box of the fridge is your first recourse, but if your ice cream container won't fit, you'll have to rethink. Let the ice cream melt (which results, effectively, in flavoured custard) and then stir in some gelatine (following the instructions on the packet). Spoon it into individual dishes, garnish them, and keep it in the fridge until you're ready to serve it.

Of course, you may be able to borrow equipment from a neighbour, or even manage without altogether. For example, you could serve pouring cream instead of whipped cream, or dice the vegetables for the soup and then leave them as they are. Even professional restaurateurs have been known to borrow their neighbour's microwave.

Dinner party excuses no.2

Vital equipment has broken

"We thought a chilled barbecue would make a change."

EEExtra guests have arrived unexpectedly

There I was, happily laying out four pieces of smoked mackerel on plates with a salad garnish, for our starter. The doorbell rang and my wife opened it. One of our guests had her mother staying so she'd brought her along too. How am I supposed to divide four smoked mackerel fillets between five?

Distraught from Durham

You're not. You're going to have to adopt a different approach to your smoked mackerel, that's all. What you need to do is get a bowl, separate the flesh from the skins, and throw away the skins (unless you have cats to give them to). Put the flesh in the bowl with a little soft butter (melt it if it's hard and you're in a hurry) and some black pepper. Mush the whole lot together and, hey presto, you've made smoked mackerel pâté. Just divide it into five, toast five or ten slices of bread (with the crusts cut off) and serve it with the salad garnish.

Of course, there's a chance that extra guests may turn up when you're serving something other than smoked mackerel fillets. You probably know of certain people who are more likely than others to bring extra people without warning, and it would be rash to plan a meal that couldn't stretch when you're expecting this kind of guest. But even if you think ahead like this, there will still be the occasional dinner guests who surprise you by bringing a friend. So what do you do if you're serving individual syllabubs for pudding, or chicken breast portions for main course?

There are two basic approaches to this problem, at least one of which should apply to any problem caused by thoughtless guests turning up without warning you that they're bringing someone else:

● chop everything up

● pool it

Let's look at each approach with a few examples, and you'll see how simple it is.

Chop everything up

So you can't divide six chicken breasts between seven people. Just chop each one into three or four smaller pieces. I know this still isn't divisible by seven, but if you make the pieces different sizes you can give people either two large or three small pieces. This works for loads of different dishes such as meat, fruit (divide whole poached oranges into segments), vegetables (four or six mini cauliflowers can be split into lots of florets), and so on. If you keep an emergency supply of ready-made puff pastry (see page 103) you can make an individual lid for each dish of combined ingredients.

THINKING AHEAD

If you're planning to make individual portions of anything that you can't later divide – vegetable tartlets, sponge pud-

dings or whatever – always make a couple of extras. Even if you don't get extra guests without warning, one of the dishes may get dropped, the pudding will fail to turn out, or one of them won't set properly.

Pool it

When a dish is hard to divide without it being obvious what you're up to, you can often just combine the whole thing. The smoked mackerel pate was an example of this. But take something like baked apples. You can't very well chop these into quarters, but you could spoon the cooked flesh from all of them into a single dish and top it with whipped cream. Or cover it in peaks of whisked egg white with a bit of sugar in and stick it back in the oven for a few minutes to make 'apple snow'.

A roast that is no longer big enough to go round the assembled multitude can be turned into a stew or curry at the last minute. This should help to swell the quantity, too, by the time you've added a few chopped onions or carrots or whatever. And you can always eke it out further by cooking extra rice or potatoes to go with it.

If you've made individual dishes, such as syllabubs, you can just decant them all back into a communal serving bowl and top it off with an appropriate garnish. A dollop of whipped cream and some lemon zest would do for syllabubs. Even something like an avocado starter can be made to stretch: cube the avocado flesh with some skinned tomatoes, a few almonds if you have them, some fried up lardons of bacon or anything else that comes to hand, and serve the 'avocado salad' in individual dishes.

Or, of course, you can take the truly assertive approach and shut the door in the face of your extra guest, pointing out that you don't offer your hospitality to rude, inconsiderate people. The atmosphere may suffer for the rest of the evening if you take this option, but it's your choice.

Dinner party excuses no.19

Extra guests have arrived unexpectedly.

"We're going to play a game, everyone. It's like musical chairs but it's called musical puddings."

Your guests forgot to tell you about their *special* diet

I cooked a really good casserole, with lyonnaise potatoes and vegetables, followed by individual rice puddings. When two of our four guests arrived they said, "Whoops, forgot to tell you, we're on the Atkins" (whatever that is). We'll just eat meat and vegetables. They then cross-examined me about the contents of the casserole – which contained, apparently, three absolute no-nos: flour, swede and parsnips. "Never mind," I said, floundering, "you can have extra vegetables." However they turned down my delicious lyonnaise potatoes, and the Vichy carrots. All they could eat was a plate of runner beans. And after all that, they wouldn't touch the rice puddings either. I was really pissed off, but I couldn't help feeling dreadful about not giving them a decent supper. I'd spent most of the afternoon putting together what I thought was a good meal for them.

Unappreciated from Uttoxeter

It's my personal view that anyone who forgets to tell their host about special dietary requirements should be made to eat what's put in front of them as a lesson to prevent them doing it to anyone else in future. Moreover I would extend this rule to cover people who fondly imagine that their eating foibles are so important to you that you have remembered them from the last time they came to dinner.

Every time you are invited to a meal you should remind the hosts that you are vegetarian, allergic to mushrooms, an orthodox Jew, on the cabbage soup diet or whatever it is. And if the diet is in the least difficult to accommodate, you should bring your own food.

If guests tell you too late about their special requirements that's frankly their problem, not yours. You have every right to make them sit and starve all evening. However, most of us have a generous desire to feed our guests well even if they are making it difficult. We start out to give everyone a good evening with delicious food and we're reluctant to abandon that aim. And we want to be seen as a calm and willing provider who will happily fit round completely unreasonable demands at the last minute.

So what can you do? Well, here are a few suggestions:

● *Give them more of what they **can** eat* If someone's diet is so restrictive they can eat very little, the chances are that they will have remembered to warn you. The most common restrictive diet that people don't warn you about is vegetarianism. I sometimes think that it's down to the vegetarians' smugness, that they think everyone ought to eat that way anyway, and you're the one with the unreasonable diet. (That remark was completely unfair, obviously, and I know lots of vegetarians who are entirely humble about their personal dietary choices. But I have met a fair few smug ones too...)

Anyway, just cook some extra vegetables if you have them, and pile them up on the vegetarians' plates. If you keep emergency puff pastry (see page 103) you can cook a lid to go on the top. Or give second helpings of pudding to the person who couldn't eat much of the main course (bearing in mind that vegetarians can't eat gelatine). This not only means that they get well fed despite everything, it should also mean they feel doubly guilty about not forewarning you of their diet. You can pile on the guilt along with the vegetables with comments such as, "There's just enough pudding left over for one person to have seconds. Sorry, folks, but I'd better give it to Diana since she's barely eaten, poor thing." That'll help her remember to tell future hosts about her picky eating habits.

- *Adapt the recipe* This isn't always possible, but don't forget to consider it. If your guest is allergic to dairy products, for example, and you were going to thicken the sauce with cream at the end of the cooking process, thicken it with flour instead. If they arrive before you've stirred the cream into the fruit purée, serve the fruit and cream separately. Depending on the diet, there are often minor adjustments you can make if you're willing to be flexible which will extend the foods your guest can eat.

- *Lie* You can always tell your guests that there is no flour in the casserole, or that you didn't roast the potatoes in the meat fat when you actually did. Personally, I would never take this option dealing with someone whose dietary requirements were driven by religion or genuine allergy. Obviously you can't tell someone with an anaphylactic reaction to nuts that a meal is nut free when it isn't, just to retaliate for them not warning you about their allergy before you started cooking. But I must confess I have served well disguised mushrooms to someone who claimed a mushroom allergy which I knew was imaginary (and they never knew, nor suffered any symptoms). It's really up to you, and quite an interesting question, actually – the sort of truth game you might play after a good meal: would you lie to a vegan and tell them you had cooked the pastry with vegetarian suet when you hadn't?

THINKING AHEAD

This potential disaster is a good example of the value of keeping a meal or two ready in your freezer for emergencies (see page 106). Vegetarian meals are particularly handy, as you can also serve them to non-vegetarians.

A second meal from scratch

If none of these options is feasible and, as in the example above, there's very little your guests can actually eat, your best bet is to throw together a quick, tasty and filling dish to serve alongside the main meal. It's a pain, of course, and it probably won't be quite as delicious as the rest of the meal, but boy will it make you look good.

Most people can eat rice (apart from Atkins people, who *can* eat it but won't). It's fine if you're vegetarian, vegan, or a follower of any religion that I know of, and I've never heard of a rice allergy. Your store cupboard should always contain rice for emergencies (see page 103), and ideally you'll have some kind of risotto rice. If you're nervous about cooking rice, see page 77. You can throw together a risotto by adding whatever ingredients are permitted by the diet in question. For example:

- chopped vegetables (whatever you have in the kitchen)
- nuts (so long as your guest isn't a nut allergy sufferer)
- tinned vegetables (sweetcorn, tomatoes, mushrooms)
- meat (if you have any left unsullied, or you could donate tomorrow night's supper)
- prawns (if you happen to have any; frozen is fine)

Just chuck the whole lot in with the rice while it's cooking. Make sure there's only enough water to cover and keep topping it up as necessary – that way you won't have to strain any of it off at the end and chuck the flavour away with it. Add some liquid stock or a stock cube if the diet allows it. When it's cooked, toss in some butter and serve it with grated cheese on the side (assuming your guest doesn't have a dairy allergy).

An alternative method is to fry all the ingredients except the rice. Cook the rice separately, strain it and then add it to the pan. Heat it through and season it.

The timing goes all wrong:-

I was cooking a meal which I was really pleased with, right up to the last minute. The meat was cooked, the potatoes and runner beans dished up, the sauce ready... but the damn broccoli wouldn't cook. By the time it was ready everything else was either getting cold out of the oven or going dry in it. I was so upset.

Disappointed from Devon

It's always the bloody broccoli in my experience. That's because I steam it; it cooks much faster, of course, if you put it straight in the water. Actually, getting everything ready at the same time is arguably the toughest part of cooking for guests. There are things you can do when it happens, but long term it's also worth knowing how to minimise the risk of it happening at all.

Cure

If you find yourself with half the meal ready to go and the other half not yet cooked, it doesn't help to be told how you might have prevented it if you'd thought ahead. So here are some tips that might help if you're in trouble:

● Put anything you can in a low oven to keep warm. Put butter on vegetables, and a lid or cover over them, to prevent them drying out.

- Speed up the offending item of food in some way. For example, take the broccoli off the stove, cut the stems off, and put it back on to cook quicker. Or take it out of the steamer and put it into a pan of boiling water (the one at the bottom of the steamer will do nicely). Or cut up meat into smaller pieces.

- Abandon the thing. This doesn't work for the main dish, but you might be able to give up on one vegetable and never mention that you'd planned to serve it.

- Wait. Maybe it doesn't matter that much if you're more flexible about the timing. Just delay the start of the meal. If the pudding is cooking slower than you thought just take a longer break between courses. Lots of people do it anyway; just let your guests think you're the kind of people who go in for long, relaxed meals.

- If things get a bit cold, you can often disguise it by making sure you serve any sauce or gravy piping hot.

- If the meal is delayed, find something to serve as a pre-meal snack – a bag of Bombay mix or a packet of crisps (see page 103). Not only does it keep people happy, it also gives the impression that you always meant to serve the meal later.

Prevention

If you have a persistent problem with timing (and lots of us do) there are ways to minimise the risk. Even if you want to learn to perfect the timing thing, at least you can take these preventative measures for the occasional meal that you really want to get right.

- Steam your vegetables. The point of this is that if something else slows you down you can keep the vegetable water simmering lightly in the steamer and the vegetables won't lose their flavour or their colour in the way they would if you overcooked them in water.

- ...apart from broccoli. I'm very fond of the stuff, but it does seem to be one of the most frequent culprits when timing goes wrong. It's fine if you cook it in boiling water, but if you steam it, it somehow always takes longer than you could possibly expect.

- Serve salad instead of vegetables.

Dinner party excuses no.27

The timing goes all wrong

"I thought pudding first, then main course. Apparently it's the latest thing on the left bank."

- Cook what you can in advance so it has only to heat through and not actually cook from scratch.

** If you're cooking anything that won't overcook, put it in early so it can't undercook, leaving you juggling the rest of the meal while you wait for it. In other words if you're cooking, say, Moroccan braised lamb shank which is supposed to take three hours, you know perfectly well that it will taste even better after four hours. So put it in four hours before you eat and you can be even more confident that it will be ready on time.

SALVAGE SECRETS

Just because you knew when you invited your guests for 8pm that you planned to eat at 8.30, it doesn't mean *they* know it. If things go wrong, just give yourself more time. Eat at 9pm instead – they won't know any different. The same applies to how long a break you take between courses.

Part 2

Notorious problems *and* how to put them right

Potatoes

We had some rather posh new friends over to supper. We'd been to them once and they'd served up a delicious meal. So I wanted to do the same. The dinner turned out how I wanted it to apart from the mashed potato, which was all lumpy. It's such a basic dish, for goodness sake, I felt awful that I couldn't get it right.

Amateur from Accrington

For a staple food which most of us cook frequently, it's surprising how often potatoes fail to turn out as we'd intended. The mash is lumpy, the roasties won't brown or the boiled potatoes have broken up. All these problems are curable, however, and here are some ideas for dealing with them, along with some tips for preventing them in future.

Mashed potato

The problem with mashed potato is lumps. Getting them flavoursome is easy – you just keep adding butter and seasoning – but you want to know how to get the lumps out. It's actually very straightforward, if a little tedious: push the potato through a sieve (or a fine ricer if you have one). By the time you've done that it will be cold, so put it in the oven in a dish with a lid, with some butter on the top of the potato, and heat it through before you serve it.

If you think the lumpiness isn't bad enough to warrant this effort, try beating the mash with a wooden spoon, which often does the trick.

Another trick is to fry up a few onions and rosemary, add them to the lumpy potatoes and put the whole lot through the blender. The few small lumps that remain will be mistaken for onion, and the whole thing will taste delicious.

It won't help once the potatoes are mashed and lumpy but, for next time, you can make sure the potatoes are cooked thoroughly by taking one of them out and mashing it well with a fork as a test. You'll also find that it helps to mash the potato *before* you add any liquid such as butter or cream.

Roast potatoes

Roast potatoes that won't brown are a pain. If they're almost ready, a knob of butter in with them will add some colour by burning. You can move them up to the top of a hot oven of course, but you've probably tried that already. Or maybe you need the oven cooler for something else. In that case, take the potatoes out of the oven altogether and deep fry them on top of the cooker.

If you want to know the secret of good, crispy roast potatoes, here it is. Parboil the potatoes for six or seven minutes first (in stock if you want to add flavour) and then drain them. Let them dry out well and then shake them in the pan so the edges start to break up slightly. Now you can put them in a roasting pan of pre-heated oil or fat and roast as normal.

Boiled potatoes

The problem with boiled potatoes is when they break up. If this happens, drain them and mash them. If they are new potatoes boiled in their skins, crush them with the back of a spoon. Serve them with plenty of butter and a touch of black pepper and tell your guests they are 'crushed potatoes' (which they are). This is a fashionable way to serve potatoes and, more to the point, it will look intentional.

Dauphinois potatoes

These are those potatoes which you slice, place in a shallow dish, cover in cream and bake in the oven. There are lots of variations, mostly involving cheese or onions. The recipe usually suggests optimistically that you should cook them for around an hour. However, I have known them take as long as five hours, and I have many friends whose experiences have driven them never to cook the dish at all (a shame, since it's quite delicious when it works).

If you get caught out, you can put the dish in the microwave to cook the potatoes through. If you don't have a microwave, pour off any excess cream and sauté the potatoes in a frying pan. The remaining traces of cream and/or cheese will brown nicely.

If you want to prevent the problem happening again, the answer is to just cook the potatoes gently by boiling on top of the stove before you start. Then slice them, pour the cream over and carry on as normal.

THINKING AHEAD

One of the basic principles of cooking potatoes is to start with the right variety. Some potatoes will never roast well, and others are always lumpy when you mash them, or never

get crispy skins when they're baked. If you buy your potatoes in the supermarket, read the label on the bag which will tell you what they're suitable for. If you buy them at a proper old-fashioned greengrocer, just ask for advice. Don't think they're 'only spuds' and you can get away with buying the cheapest. The best varieties really do taste better.

Rice

I cooked the best curry ever – I was really pleased with it – and all I had to do was cook the rice to go with it. The easy bit, I thought. How wrong I was. The stuff all stuck together in one gooey lump and when I tried to separate it with a fork I couldn't. I had to serve it up all gungy. I was so disappointed I burst into tears.

Mournful from Manchester

What is it with these basic, staple foods like rice and potatoes? They can be so hard to get right. There are two classic disaster areas with rice: it sticks together, or it burns on the bottom of the pan. Fortunately, both of these can be salvaged.

Sticky rice

The thing about rice is that it contains a lot of starch which is what makes it sticky. The more thoroughly you rinse the rice before you cook it, the better. But it's no good telling you that now, of course. You want to know what to do after you didn't rinse it first and it's too late.

Well, you can always rinse it afterwards. Put the lump of stuck together rice in a sieve or a colander and run it under the cold tap. This should help separate the grains and rinse out the starch. Finish by pouring boiling water over it to reheat it. If the rice was very sticky and the process has taken so long it's stone cold, put it back into boiling water for a couple of minutes to heat through.

If you feel the rice has passed the point where you can salvage it even this way, you can make a virtue out of adversity. Form the rice into small balls (easy when it's in this state) and deep fry them. You could even put some cheese in the centre of each one which will melt as you fry the rice. Dish up the meal with rice balls on the side and everyone will be really impressed.

For next time, try adding a spoonful of lemon juice to the water you boil the rice in. Don't ask me why but it helps reduce stickiness. Use a big pan with lots of water, and do your best to avoid boiling the rice too fast.

Burnt rice

There are two problems here. One is that all the rice can taste slightly burnt when the bottom of the pan burns, and the other is that some of the rice is unusable. The first thing to do is to take a slice of bread (trust me here) and lay it on the top of the rice in the pan. Put a lid on it and leave it to stand for about ten minutes. The bread soaks up a lot of the burnt taste, and you can then throw it away.

Now you need to resist the temptation to spoon all the rice furiously into a dish while cursing and blaming the cooker, the pan, the phone call you took when you should have been turning the rice down, and all the rest of it. In fact, even if the bread trick had no effect whatever it would still be worthwhile just for making you chill for ten minutes.

You need to spoon the rice out of the pan carefully so that none of the burnt rice comes out with it. Any rice that is borderline should be rejected – even if it looks OK, it will taste burnt. You should, however, be able to salvage most of the rice. If there really isn't enough to go round, cook more if you have enough, obviously, or bulk out some other part of the meal so your guests don't go hungry.

By the way, if you put the rice in the pan before the water was boiling, you have only yourself to blame really if it sticks to the bottom and burns. You need to wait until the water is boiling properly, and give the rice a quick stir as you put it in.

Dinner party excuses no.69

The rice is burnt

"We found this curry recipe in Calcutta last time we were there, where the locals always serve it with breadcrumbs instead of rice."

THINKING AHEAD

As with potaotes, there are lots of different kinds of rice. Each one is intended for a different purpose. While you obviously don't *have* to use them in the way suggested – you're a grown up and you can be as creative as you like – it will reduce problems if you use the right type of rice.

Generally speaking, round-grained rices such as pudding rice and risotto rice are stickier than the long grained varieties. If you're cooking a risotto it should be regularly stirred so it won't stick. However, if you look in your cupboard and find you have only a round grained rice of some kind to cook with your curry, and you then plunge it in boiling water and ignore it for 20 minutes, you really are asking for trouble.

Long-grain rice is the least likely to stick since it contains less starch. Personally I use basmati rice when I feel it remotely goes with the dish I'm cooking, since it's never gone sticky on me. Again, it's a long-grain variety and less starchy.

Pastry——⌐

*My puff pastry didn't puff! I've never seen anything less puffy.
It was flat, wet pastry. It ruined a good beef Wellington.*

Sunk from Sudbury

Puff pastry is notoriously temperamental. Even shortcrust pastry can be very variable, although the results if it fails aren't quite so dramatic. In my experience, the best bet if it all goes horribly wrong is to remove the pastry altogether so no one knows it was ever meant to be there. If bits of it are left around the edge of the dish, just swap dishes.

Sometimes you have time to replace it. Or you can replace it with something different. For example:

- A steak and kidney pie could be topped with sliced potatoes instead – obviously you'd have to rename it 'beef hotpot' or something.

- An apple pie with no pastry can be topped with whisked egg whites and sugar and put back in the oven to brown. This actually has a name already: apple snow (but hey, make up a new one if you like).

- Vol-au-vent fillings can be put on toast instead. Let's call them chicken and mushroom croûtes. That sounds good. If you know the French for 'chicken and mushroom' you can make them sound even more fancy.

- If your pastry has shrunk away from the edges of the dish, serve individual portions rather than bringing the whole dish to the table, and they'll never know.

You get the picture. Or, best of all, you can have a secret stash of ready-made pastry to use in emergencies (see page 103).

Salvage secrets

Ready-made pastry is, of course, your secret weapon here. Even if you want to have a crack at making your own puff pastry, it's still worth having as a fallback. It's even useful for rescuing dishes that didn't originally include pastry at all. A square or round of puff pastry – cooked individually – can sit on top of many a dish that's gone wrong and hide the evidence. Or it can bulk out the meal when some of the other ingredients turn out to be unusable for any reason (they've gone off, the cat has eaten them, your guests refuse to eat them).

Advance planning

For next time – or if you've thought to read this in advance of cooking a pastry-related dish – here's a couple of tips to minimise any potential disaster:

- If you make your own pastry, try to make it well in advance and cook some of it ahead of time as a test. I'm reluctant to make guarantees here, but generally if the test piece rises well, so will the main batch (so long as you don't mess with it in the interim).

- If possible, cook the pastry separately from the rest of the dish. You can add it as a lid before serving. This makes it much easier to salvage any problems – the main dish is unsullied by burnt or unrisen pastry – and if the pastry is ready first you can take it out of the oven instead of having to leave it to burn because it's attached to the uncooked other half of the meal.

Soggy choux pastry

Choux pastry doesn't often give you trouble making it. The only problem you're likely to encounter is that it can go soggy if you make it ahead of time. If this happens, just put it back in a medium oven for a few minutes to dry it out again. (This works for soggy meringues too.)

Dinner party excuses no.33

The pastry has shrunk

"This is stewed apple served with a pastry isle flottante."

Shortcrust pastry

If your shortcrust pastry cooks OK but is usually a bit tough, you might like to know the secret of melt-in-your-mouth short-crust. Actually, to be honest, I'm only putting this in as a chance to brag; it isn't really anything to do with salvaging disasters. You know how all of us has at least one thing we can cook really brilliantly? Well, mine is shortcrust pastry so I'm going to tell you the trick. If you're not interested in listening to people showing off, please feel free to skip on to the next section.

There are three secrets to good shortcrust and, in combination, they're irresistible:

- Use self-raising flour, despite what the recipe books say.
- Use all lard (or the vegetarian equivalent) instead of half butter; it makes it really light.
- Use slightly less water than the very least you think you can get away with.

There. I've got that out of my system. You can go on to the next page now.

Gravy

I dished up a Sunday roast for friends the other day, but the gravy was all thin and watery and tasted of almost nothing. Where did I go wrong, and how could I have saved it?

Wishy-washy from Warrington

Lumps. That's the usual problem you get with gravy. So you're doing well if wateriness is all you have to complain about. What you want is to turn your lumpy bland liquid into smooth, flavoursome gravy. The other problems you may encounter with gravy are being too thick or too thin.

Losing the lumps

The way to do this is simply to pour the gravy through a sieve. What could be simpler? You should be able to push the lumpy bits through and break them up in the process. If you don't have a wire sieve, whisk the gravy with a birch twig whisk if you have one, use a stick blender, or put the whole lot in the blender (but don't make the mistake of filling it too full with hot gravy; it could erupt and burn you).

Gaining flavour

The easiest way to add taste to watery gravy is to put in half a stock cube or some liquid stock. To be honest, it's not quite as good as making the gravy well flavoured in the first place (see below), but it's perfectly serviceable and much better than leaving it as it is.

Too thick?

If the gravy being too thick is a problem, presumably you've run out of good tasty liquid to add, otherwise it wouldn't be a problem. If you need suitable liquid to add, just open up a tin of vegetables (just about any kind will do) and add the water from that.

Too thin?

Obviously you can put some fat and flour in a pan, cook them together to make a roux (sorry, bit of jargon sneaked in there) and add your thin gravy gradually, stirring all the while to make sure it doesn't turn lumpy on you (if it does, go back three spaces and miss a turn). But this takes time, just at that stage of the meal when you don't want to insert an extra five minutes into the proceedings. There are two things you can do. Either mix up a little cornflour and water until it's smooth and add it slowly to the gravy, stirring all the time. Or, if you have it, add a sprinkling of instant potato to thicken it up.

Gravy principles

If you want plenty of gravy you generally need to thicken the meat juices with flour and then add more liquid which in turn thins the gravy down and gives you more of it. There are certain things you need to know in order to get gravy to work:

- Thickening the gravy with flour works in the same way as making, say, a white sauce: you combine the fat and the flour and then slowly add the liquid.

- This means that you need some fat to absorb the flour. And you need roughly the right proportion of fat to flour. The best fat to use is the fat in the meat pan. If there's too much you can pour some of it off. You need enough flour to absorb all the fat you have, otherwise there will be fat floating on top of the gravy. Add less rather than more if you're uncertain, and then add small quantities until you can see all the fat has been absorbed.

- Cook the fat and flour together before adding any more liquid – just boil away for a couple of minutes. Then add the liquid slowly so that you can combine it smoothly with the fat/flour mixture before adding more.

- The gravy will be as flavoursome as the liquid that goes into it. Best of all are the juices from the pan you roasted the meat in. Ideally, make the gravy in this pan so you can get all the flavour into it. Let your joint stand and wrap it in foil: more juices will emerge as the meat relaxes. If you carve the meat a few minutes in advance and keep it on a hot dish, even more juices will run out to add to your gravy.

- If you have giblets, cook these up and add the cooking liquor to the gravy.

- Next best after this is the water from your vegetables. If you generally steam vegetables, cook something tasty (such as broccoli or runner beans) in water so you have some flavoursome liquid to add. This is just as healthy as steaming because you're not going to lose any nutrients – they'll just be in the gravy instead of the vegetables. Make sure you have enough vegetable water so you never have to add anything less tasty, such as tap water. That's when your gravy will start to lose its flavour.

- If you don't have any fresh vegetable water to add, just add tinned vegetable water.

- Failing this, you'll have to use water but you can prevent the gravy losing flavour by adding some liquid stock concentrate or part of a stock cube.

Sauces

I decided to make a hollandaise sauce to go with the poached salmon I was doing. I've made it before. It was all going really well and then suddenly, for no reason, it curdled. I had to serve mayonnaise from a jar instead, and I was so disappointed.

Saucy from Shrewsbury

Hollandaise sauce does this occasionally. I think it's just a bloody-minded sauce, although professional chefs insist there's a good reason for it. Mayonnaise is another one which lulls you into a false sense of security and then splits on you.

A lot of sauces are pretty straightforward. It's hard to go far wrong with apple sauce or bread sauce (I'll regret writing that). However, here are some guidelines on rescuing three of the most wilful: hollandaise, mayonnaise and béchamel.

Hollandaise

This is a delicious sauce, and you can't fail to impress guests by making it yourself – assuming it all goes right. What's more, the home-made version is far superior to any packaged variety I've ever tasted. You'd serve hollandaise with hot fish or vegetables, or in Eggs Benedict. A classic variation on hollandaise, called béarnaise, is flavoured with tarragon and chervil and served with grilled meat and fish.

A hollandaise is similar to a warm mayonnaise. You start with whisked egg yolks and a bit of vinegar, and you add liquid fat (in this case melted butter) gradually. As this combines with the egg yolks it thickens to a similar consistency to mayonnaise.

The trouble is, it has this nasty habit of curdling just when you least expect it. It doesn't have the decency to warn you that it's thinking of curdling. Just bam! and it's gone. However, there are two ways to salvage it.

Either start again with fresh egg yolks, and gradually whisk in the curdled sauce in place of fresh butter. Or put a teaspoon of boiling water in a pan and gradually whisk in the curdled stuff. I once had a hollandaise curdle on me five times in a row (on Christmas Eve – great time to have a bad sauce day). But I persisted, using the curdled sauce, and I eventually got the damn thing beat. The final sauce was as delicious as ever.

If you want to know what the professionals claim are the logical reasons behind hollandaise curdling, I'll tell you for next time:

- the butter has been added too fast
- the sauce has become too hot

Hollandaise tastes better made with unsalted butter. This has the added advantage that the butter contains fewer impurities, which makes the sauce less temperamental.

Mayonnaise

This is delicious home-made, and is also the basis for tartare sauce if you add chopped gherkins, capers and parsley. Like hollandaise, mayonnaise loves to catch you unawares by curdling if it senses any complacency on your part.

As with hollandaise, the answer is to put a fresh yolk in a bowl, together with about half a teaspoon of cold water, whisk it well and then gradually whisk in the curdled sauce. Or start with a tablespoon of boiling water and whisk in the curdled sauce. Again, the reconstituted sauce is indistinguishable from mayonnaise which has never curdled to begin with.

Mayonnaise is even more hard to please than hollandaise, and far too easily sulks its way to curdling if:

- you add the oil too quickly

- the oil is too cold

- you haven't whisked the sauce enough

- the yolk is stale

By the way, if mayonnaise gets too thick while you're making it you can thin it with a little vinegar.

Béchamel

This, as you probably know, is just the fancy name for white sauce. It's also the basis for cheese sauce, parsley sauce and many others. The difficulty you're likely to have with it is that it can turn lumpy if you add the milk too quickly. As with gravy (see page 85), the solution is to pass it through a wire sieve to strain out the lumps. Push the globby floury stuff through the sieve too, to break it up, and put the sauce back on the heat and carry on. Alternatively you could just put the whole lot through the blender. It adds to the washing up, but then so does the sieve. Anyway, if you're cooking, someone else should be doing the washing up (so what the hell, sieve it and blend it if you like).

THINKING AHEAD

You can cook most sauces ahead of time. This means that if it all goes wrong you have plenty of time to redo it, or to find an alternative. To put a hot sauce on one side without it forming a skin on top as it cools, cut out a circle of greaseproof paper the same size as the pan. Make a small hole in the centre (for the hot air to escape) and place the paper on the top of the sauce.

Dinner party excuses no.42

The sauce has gone lumpy

"This is chunky cheese sauce."

Part 3

Things you should know before you turn the oven on

~~Dishes~~ to avoid at all costs

Everything was going well until I got the soufflé out of the oven to serve it. I left it to stand for a couple of minutes while I sorted out the cream to go with it, and when I went to put it on the table it had collapsed.

Mortified from Montgomeryshire

Well, I'm sorry, but what on earth are you doing trying to cook a soufflé for a dinner party you really care about? You're simply asking for trouble and you deserve all you get. If you want to serve up soufflés at dinner parties, practise them endlessly on your family until you know you can get them right.

Soufflés are the classic, clichéd hard-to-cook dishes, but they are not the only meal that tempts fate. You may well have friends and family you don't mind practising on and who won't care if the meal goes wrong, but if you really want it to go right this time, cook something which isn't going to let you down.

One of the big problems with soufflés (and many other dishes) is that they have to be served the instant they come out of the oven. This means that you can't be flexible. If one of your guests decides to have a second helping of that delicious main course you cooked, and then eats very slowly, you're in trouble.

Dinner party excuses no.46

Dishes to avoid at all costs

"I was aiming for a profiterole tower in the shape of St Paul's Cathedral, but then I thought a row of bungalows would be less pretentious."

Either you leave the soufflé to burn, or you take it out whereupon it collapses. Even if your guests don't go for second helpings the phone may ring, or you may not be able to find where you put the cream, or someone may spill a glass of red wine on the tablecloth... any of these can scupper your soufflé.

The same thing, of course, applies to any other dish which requires very precise timing. Of course, it depends on your skill as a cook, and if you're sufficiently confident go ahead and cook what you like. If you're not that sure, however, avoid things like battered deep fried squid – delicious but it tastes like rubber if you give it even ten seconds too long in the pan. Fried chicken livers are much the same, needing to be just pink.

Pancakes are fine if you cook them in advance, but it's asking for trouble to cook them in front of your guests – especially the variety where you set fire to alcohol in the pan with them. Puff pastry needs to be tested in advance unless you've bought it ready made or you really know what you're doing.

And finally, don't for goodness sake cook a baked Alaska for the first time at a dinner party where you want everything to go right. If putting ice cream into a hot oven and expecting it to stay cold and hard isn't inviting trouble, I don't know what is.

THINKING AHEAD

If you're not sure a dish will work but you really want to try it, at least do a test run the day before or in the morning. And have something else on standby (see page 106) in case the whole thing goes bottom up.

Reliable dishes you can't ruin

I tried cooking a baked Alaska. It sounded so easy but I must have left it in the oven too long and it melted. Now my wife won't speak to me.

Frozen out from Falmouth

Yes, quite.

If your culinary skills aren't fully up to speed, or even if they are but your confidence is lacking, what you need is a selection of dishes which can't possibly go wrong. Or at least, are incredibly unlikely to go wrong (I don't want to get sued here). So what are the safest things to cook? Here are some ideas:

● Stews, casseroles and curries, which can cook for as long as you want them to and can't collapse, fall apart, fail to set or anything else problematic.

● Anything you can cook in advance, to give you time to put right any problems or – in extremis – start again from scratch. This obviously includes all cold dishes (excluding the middle of the baked Alaska), plus casseroles and similar dishes which can just be chilled and reheated later.

● Puddings consisting chiefly of fruit – fruit salads can look great if you use just one or two fruits, such as mango and lychee, and serve a meringue or something on the side if you want to look a bit more fancy.

And here are a couple of my personal favourites, which you might like to try:

Fruit topping

You can make a delicious topping for fruit by mixing equal quantities of whipped double cream and Greek yoghurt. Put this on top of the fruit and then sprinkle it at the last minute with dark brown sugar. Put it under the grill to caramelise the sugar.

This is terribly versatile. You can use any kind of fruit from pureéd plums to sliced bananas with lime juice. And you can serve it in individual ramekin dishes if you want it to look more fancy. In fact, even if the sugar doesn't caramelise, it's still good with sprinkled sugar. And you could add a hint of lemon juice, vanilla, cinnamon or some other flavouring to the cream/yoghurt mix.

Salamagundi

This is a real favourite. It is a deliciously over-the-top elaborate Victorian salad dish in origin, and it looks magnificent. Yet it's extremely simple to make. I've done it as the centrepiece for a wedding – it looked great and drew lots of comment, and yet I knew it couldn't go wrong.

You need a large round platter of some kind. And I mean large – around 18"/45cm across. You can buy large silver cake boards in this size and they're very inexpensive. In the middle of the board you put an upturned pudding basin or similar kind of bowl.

You need to keep your salad ingredients separate for this, and chop or slice them. You're going to arrange concentric rings of different salad foods across the whole platter. It's entirely up to you what foods you use but you might have, for example, a ring of chopped red peppers followed by a ring of sliced hard boiled egg, followed by a ring of cucumber, followed by a ring of grated cheese, and so on. Start at the middle by leaning something such as endive leaves against the side of the pudding bowl to conceal it. Then just work out until you get to the edge. When the whole dish is covered, place a small, low vase of seasonal flowers on top of the pudding bowl in the middle.

This dish just looks so impressive, and yet you haven't had to cook anything beyond the odd hard boiled egg. It's all in the assembly. Here are a few suggestions:

- Assemble the salamagundi in situ if you can. Failing that, get someone else to carry it for you in case it gets dropped. That way, it's not your fault.

- You might like to use edible flowers such as nasturtiums or primroses on the top.

- Use contrasting colours next to each other. You can mix some foods together so you might have a ring of chopped red and yellow peppers.

- You can make the dish look even more decorative if you use slices of stuffed olives or half grapes on top of other foods. So every slice of egg might have a slice of olive on top, or a ring of grated cheese might be topped off with grapes.

- It's up to you what you put in your salamagundi, but here are a few ideas: red, green, yellow and orange peppers (chopped or sliced), sliced cucumber, sliced tomatoes, radishes, chopped lettuce, olives, grapes, cheese (chopped or grated), sweetcorn, prawns, chopped ham, chopped chicken.

- Depending on how filling you make the ingredients, you can either serve the salamagundi on its own, or as an accompaniment to cold meat. Add a bowl of home-made mayonnaise (made earlier, of course) and your guests will be hugely impressed and very well fed.

Swimming salmon

Here's another deeply impressive but fiendishly simple dish, and so much more interesting than the usual poached salmon lying on its side with cucumber slices. Buy two whole salmon,

Dinner party excuses no.15

Reliable dishes you can't ruin

"Well, I thought, 'You can't go wrong with sandwiches, can you?' "

about 4-6lbs each. Lay them in the bottom of a stock pot, upright, as if they're swimming nose-to-tail. Poach them and then leave them to cool before putting them in the fridge overnight.

The next day they will have set in a vertical 'action' pose, glaring at each other and circling for position. Position them on a mirror and garnish them with the usual – lemon, parsley, shredded lettuce and grated leeks. Hide the edge of the mirror with mounds of the lettuce or leek. Top off with a little fake black and red caviar. The result is easy but impressive, with the mirror reflecting the dish and suggesting a watery setting.

Essential store cupboard first aid

The meal I was cooking went horribly wrong. I tried to salvage it but I couldn't find anything useful in the cupboard. In the end, we had to phone for a takeaway. It was so embarrassing.

Upset from Uppingham

A well stocked store cupboard is the salvation of any cook who can't guarantee perfection every time. I know I rely heavily on mine. Not only will it save you from disaster, but just having it there as a safety net will make you feel so much more secure in the kitchen. Most of it you can keep for ages, replacing only if you use it or when the long sell by date finally runs out.

There are four categories of emergency store: the fresh food store, the fridge, the freezer and the cupboard. (Possibly five if you have a well stocked vegetable and herb garden.) Unless your budget – and your storage space – is limitless you can't expect to keep every possible emergency food in the house. However all the foods on the following list are either very inexpensive, or are easily used up over the next day or two if you didn't need them. I haven't included absolute basics such as flour, sugar, salt... or we'd be here all day. I'm assuming you have those anyway.

Fresh food

- onions
- lemons
- garden herbs (preferably growing in the garden or in pots in the kitchen window)
- bread

Fridge

- butter
- double cream
- cheddar cheese
- bacon

Freezer

- ready-made puff pastry

- frozen peas (I wouldn't serve them as the only vegetable, but if the broccoli turns out to be rotting, or the cabbage is disgustingly overcooked, they are much better than nothing. Alongside another vegetable or two they're entirely acceptable.)

- ice cream (If you make your own, concoct interesting flavours such as cinnamon and numeg, or lemongrass. These make great emergency accompaniments and, at a pinch, will make a dessert on their own, especially if you add wafers or ratafia biscuits to your store cupboard.)

Cupboard

- snacks to serve if the meal is delayed – peanuts, bombay mix, crisps or whatever. The idea is to make it look as if you were always going to serve these because the meal was always intended to be later.

- rice
- pasta
- wine, red and white (you can buy quarter or third size bottles of wine at the supermarket which are ideal, or just use a dash of whatever you have opened for your guests. But don't use really cheap plonk. If you wouldn't drink it, don't cook with it.)
- tinned tomatoes
- jars of ready made sauces (preferably good quality ones) such as chicken & mushroom, or tomato & red pepper
- curry powder
- spices such as cinnamon, nutmeg, paprika, ground ginger and any particular favourites of yours
- nuts – especially blanched almonds
- gelatine
- cornflour

Dinner party excuses no.71

Essential store cupboard first aid

"What do you need – bandage? TCP? Balsamic vinegar?"

Reliable *quick* standbys and freezer meals

I cooked a delicious oriental casserole for a dinner party. Just before the guests arrived I took it out of the oven to check it and it smelt disgusting. The meat was clearly off. I had only ten minutes before they arrived so there was no time to cook anything else.

Empty-handed from Edinburgh

It's always a good idea to have the wherewithal to rustle up a quick alternative meal, just in case. Store cupboard and freezer meals are ideal because they won't go to waste if you don't need them (which will be the case most of the time).

The first thing you need is some kind of pre-meal snack in your cupboard (see page 103) with which to buy yourself time. This will give your guests something to nibble on, and give the impression that you had never planned to eat before 9pm.

Quick standbys

Your best bet for a quick meal out of the cupboard is something pasta based (just hope your guests aren't on the Atkins diet). The rule with pasta seems to be that the more sparing the sauce, the fancier the dish looks. So a thick cheese sauce poured all over it looks like a children's high tea (though it may taste delicious), while a light tossing in olive oil and pine kernels is worthy of a top class restaurant.

You can invent your own sauce, of course. Useful ingredients to add include: bacon pieces, olives, pine kernels, mushrooms, and anything finely chopped (peppers, tomatoes, broccoli – the smaller the pieces the posher the pasta will look). Toss the whole thing in olive oil or butter, and black pepper. Or cover with a sauce made of reduced double cream with some parmesan in it. An alternative to this is risotto (still no good for the Atkins people), which you can cook with much the same ingredients as the pasta.

Freezer meals

Assuming you have a freezer, you can keep spare meals permanently on standby. To make this as simple as possible:

- Don't cook especially for the freezer. Just make extra quantities of suitable meals when you're cooking them anyway, and put the extra in the freezer.

- Freeze in relatively small quantities. You may only need to defrost enough for four people, so you don't want to have frozen eight portions in one lump. Also, smaller portions will defrost quicker.

- Always label the bags. You may think you'll remember what they are but you almost certainly won't when it comes to it.

- Have something vegetarian in your freezer for that brand of vegetarian who doesn't bother to tell you about their eating habits until they arrive.

- Freeze some home-made sauces on their own. That way if the oven fails or you forget to turn it on but you still have the meat, you can simply add a sauce to it. Or you can pour the sauce over pasta. If you have a vegetarian sauce you can freeze, better still.

- Keep ready-made puff pastry in the freezer. This means you can not only heat up your casserole, but you can turn it into a very flash looking pie, or you can cook pastry squares or rounds separately and put one on top of each serving of casserole as a lid. There's no way anyone could think that was cobbled together as a last minute emergency.

Fish doesn't normally freeze very well, but here is one fun emergency dish you can make if you have some frozen white fish you can defrost. Just fry up some onions and garlic with rose-

Dinner party excuses no.82

Reliable quick standbys and freezer meals

"It's Unicef Children's Week, so fishfingers and chips alright for everyone?"

mary and thyme. Then add two tins of tomatoes. Break up the defrosted fish a bit and add it, along with a handful of diced potato. Then simply add water and plenty of tabasco. Leave it to cook for about 15 minutes while you make the accompaniments.

Serve the soup by putting the pot in the middle of the table. Also serve home-made croutons, grated cheese, and mayonnaise laced with tabasco. Your guests can assemble whatever they want on each spoonful. Tell them it's called Marseilles Fish Soup, and allude to the Moroccan influence on Marseilles dishes to explain the zing.

Worst case scenario

We had 12 friends coming over to Sunday lunch. The night before, we had a power cut and lost everything in the freezer and the fridge overnight. We came downstairs to pools of water all over the kitchen floor. The power came back on mid-morning, but then went off again just as I was about to put the meat in the (electric) oven. With all my fridge and freezer food ruined, I simply couldn't put together a decent meal.

Powerless from Prestatyn

OK, you win. There are times when there really isn't anything you can do to salvage the meal. With everything we've covered up to this point it should be extremely rare, but just occasionally you have to admit defeat. You still have 12 friends turning up, however, and they will still be hungry. So what can you do?

If the weather is decent, you may have the kind of meal you can adapt to barbecue cooking. Assuming you have a barbecue, this is one solution which will still enable you to conceal the disaster from your guests.

Another possible option, with a reasonable enough budget, is to announce when your friends turn up, "Surprise! We thought we'd take you out to dinner for a change."

However, there are those rare times when you will have to 'fess up. And why not? It's hardly your fault. Blame it on the electricity company, and tell your guests a sob story about your freezer food being ruined and you spending all morning clearing up. You'll get loads of sympathy. After all, you'd be totally understanding if you were the guest.

However, don't sound sorry for yourself or play the martyr. Be stoical and see the funny side of it. That way you can rally your guests to treat it as a culinary adventure. See if you can persuade them all to eat beans on toast (OK, beans on bread), or whatever you have in your cupboards. Or phone for a pizza or some other kind of food if you can (not an option in more rural parts of the country, as I know only too well). Or head off to the shops to buy salad. I have one friend who, following a major kitchen disaster, treated all his friends to fish and chips and champagne.

THINKING AHEAD

The sooner you can admit defeat the better, in this kind of crisis. If you stand around forlornly hoping the electricity will come back on you may well be unlucky. But if you can recognise potential disaster you may catch it early enough to avert it. You might have time to nip out to the shops, or phone one of your friends and ask them to call in at the supermarket on their way over. You'll have to rethink the meal, of course, but that shouldn't be a problem.

One of the most delicious meals is a table covered with cheeses, good bread, fruit, cold meat, olives and so on, all arranged attractively on plates and dishes. You need no equipment at all to prepare this – no cooker, no fridge – and so long as someone has time to get to the shops you can always lay on this kind of meal. You can even light a bonfire in order to cook jacket potatoes to go with it if you want something hot. In fact, you can cook anything in the bonfire so long as you smother it in garlic and olive oil and triple wrap it in foil. Turn it when you can get near enough. This even works for large joints of meat or whole chickens.

The important thing is to have fun with it rather than make it sound like a disaster. That way your guests may not get the lunch they were expecting, but they'll still get good company and a fun time – and *something* to eat – which is what they came for. If you allow the atmosphere to be ruined along with the food, that's when you really let them down.

Dinner party excuses no.47

Worst case scenario: total failure and how to cope

"We've converted to a little-known New Age sect which holds that all food just encourages dependency."

Never forget that the reason your guests come round is to see you and enjoy your company. The food is a bonus. If that was all they wanted, they could have gone out to a restaurant on their own. So as long as you don't starve them, you can still give them a good time, not to mention providing a great story they can dine out on for years.

Contact us

You're welcome to contact White Ladder Press if you have any questions or comments for either us or the author. Please use whichever of the following routes suits you.

Phone 01803 813343 between 9am and 5.30pm

Email enquiries@whiteladderpress.com

Fax 01803 813928

Address: White Ladder Press, Great Ambrook, Near Ipplepen, Devon TQ12 5UL

Website www.whiteladderpress.com

Could you be a barker?

No, we're not casting aspersions on your character. We mean Barker in the sense of town crier or advocate. Our White Ladder Barkers spread the word and build themselves a business (part time or full time is up to you) while they do it.

We're always keen to find enthusiastic and motivated people who want to earn some money – or fundraise for a local school or favourite charity – by selling our books. The deal's very simple. We provide the books at a healthy discount, and you sell them on at full price and keep the difference. There's a modest minimum order of £30. You can sell on an ongoing basis, on stalls at events such as school fairs, coffee mornings or business get-togethers, and you can organise events and parties to sell the books.

Our books are fun, quirky and genuinely useful, and many of your customers will have seen the extensive press coverage the books get. So they're easy to sell and, because they're fun (and often funny), they're a great talking point with friends and customers.

Once you decide you like the idea of being a Barker, call Richard on 01803 814124 and he'll sort you out with your first consignment of books. We'd love you to join us.

Full Time Father

HOW TO SUCCEED AS A STAY AT HOME DAD

"At last, a hands-on, amusing and above all realistic guide for dads who have given up work to bring up their children. What makes this book so rewarding is that it is written by a father who has been there, seen it and done it."
Nick Cavender, Chairman, HomeDad UK

So your partner earns more than you do?
You've been made redundant? You hate the job?
Being a full time dad can make a lot of sense.

But isn't it a bit weird? Actually no; it's a growing trend. Nearly one in ten fathers in the UK now takes the main responsibility for looking after the kids, often full time.

It's a big decision though. What will your mates think? Will you ever get a decent job again? Won't you miss the cut and thrust of the office? And won't you go stark staring mad without any mental stimulation too sophisticated for a toddler? It's not just you, either. It's the whole family set up. Who wears the trousers? Who controls the family purse? And does it mean you have to clean the house and do the shopping, too?

Full Time Father is written by a stay at home dad and draws on his survey of other 'homedads' as well as on his own experience. It examines all the key issues, passes on masses of valuable tips and advice, and lets the reader know what to expect – both good and bad – should they decide to become a homedad themselves.

OUT OF YOUR TOWNIE MIND

THE REALITY BEHIND THE DREAM OF COUNTRY LIVING

"Richard Craze yanks the rose-tinted spectacles from the rural idyll and tramples them in the mud. The result is cheeky but charming – a kind of Feel-the-Fear-But-Do-It-Anyway for wannabe downshifters."
Hugh Fearnley-Whittingstall

We all have our own fantasy of what life in the country will be like. But are we right? Is it all roses round the door, or are they really brambles?

So you're finally sick of city life. You close your eyes and dream of living in the country – all that space, and wonderful views. Going for long walks and coming home to an open fire, bringing your children up healthy and safe and being part of a community. Maybe you have visions of baking cakes on an Aga, keeping your own hens and handknitting your own yoghurt…

But will it really be like that?

Out of Your Townie Mind takes the most popular dreams of rural life that townies have (based on a survey of aspiring country dwellers) and lays the real facts on the line. Does a big garden really give you more space to enjoy the country, or just create so much work you never have time to enjoy it? Will a house in the woods be a private haven of wildlife, your own nature reserve on the doorstep… or is it just dark, damp and a recipe for endless gutter clearing?

Out of Your Townie Mind shows you how, with a bit of forethought, you can get the very best out of country living by avoiding the pitfalls other townies stumble into.

KIDS&Co

"Ros Jay has had a brilliant idea, and what is more she has executed it brilliantly. **KIDS & CO** is the essential handbook for any manager about to commit the act of parenthood, and a thoroughly entertaining read for everyone else"
JOHN CLEESE

WHEN IT COMES TO RAISING YOUR KIDS, YOU KNOW MORE THAN YOU THINK.

So you spent five or ten years working before you started your family? Maybe more? Well, don't waste those hard-learned skills. Use them on your kids. Treat your children like customers, like employees, like colleagues.

No, really.

Just because you're a parent, your business skills don't have to go out of the window when you walk in throughthe front door. You may sometimes feel that the kids get the better of you every time, but here's one weapon you have that they don't: all those business skills you already have and they know nothing about. Closing the sale, win/win negotiating, motivational skills and all the rest.

Ros Jay is a professsional author who writes on both business and parenting topics, in this case simultaneously. She is the mother of three young children and stepmother to another three grown-up ones.

THE VOICE OF TOBACCO

"An amazing new book on smoking – it has great style and humour, and is brilliantly funny. Read this happy smoker's guide – if only I had been the author."
LESLIE PHILLIPS

What does the Voice of Tobacco say to you?
There's no need to give up; just cutting down will do.
How can it be bad for you when it feels so good?
Just one cigarette can't hurt you, now can it?
It's hard not to listen. Especially when, from the other side of the debate, we smokers have all been lectured by self-righteous prigs who think that (a) we should want to give up and (b) giving up smoking should be easy.
Well we don't and it ain't.
And yet there does come a time when, no matter how much we enjoy smoking, we have to become not smokers.
Richard Craze's guide gives it to you straight: what it's really like to give up smoking. The headaches, the sleeplessness, the irritability. And The Voice. He's been there and his diary reports back from the front line. It may not be pleasant, but it's honest. It may or may not help you to give up smoking, but it will certainly get you looking at smoking in a new way. And it will give you something to do with your hands.

This is the diary of a dedicated and happy smoker who is now not smoking. Here's how he did it. Here's how to do it without the trauma, the withdrawal symptoms, the twitching, the bad temper. Yeah, right. In your dreams.

The White Ladder Diaries

"To start a business from scratch with a great idea but little money is a terrifying but thrilling challenge. White Ladder is a fine example of how sheer guts and drive can win the day." **TIM WATERSTONE**

Have you ever dreamed of starting your own business?

Want to know what it's like? I mean, what it's really like?

Ros Jay and her partner, Richard Craze, first had the idea for White Ladder Press in the summer of 2002. This is the story of how they overcame their doubts and anxieties and brought the company to life, for only a few thousand pounds, and set it on its way to being a successful publishing company (this is its third book).

The White Ladder Diaries isn't all theory and recollections. It's a real life, day-by-day diary of all those crucial steps, naïve mistakes and emotional moments between conceiving the idea for a business and launching the first product. It records the thinking behind all the vital decisions, from choosing a logo or building a website, to sorting out a phone system or getting to grips with discounts.

What's more, the diary is littered with tips and advice for anyone else starting up a business. Whether you want to know how to register a domain name or how to write a press release, it's all in here.

If they could do it, so can you. Go on – stop dreaming. Be your own boss.

Babies for Beginners

If it isn't in here, you don't need to know it.

At last, here is the book for every new parent who's never been quite sure what a cradle cap is and whether you need one. **Babies for Beginners** cuts the crap – the unnecessary equipment, the over-fussy advice – and gives you the absolute basics of babycare: keep the baby alive, at all costs, and try to stop it getting too hungry.

From bedtime to bathtime, mealtime to playtime, this book highlights the CORE OBJECTIVE of each exercise (for example, get the baby bathed) and the KEY FOCUS (don't drown it). By exploding the myths around each aspect of babycare, the book explains what is necessary and what is a bonus; what equipment is essential and what you can do without.

Babies for Beginners is the perfect book for every first time mother who's confused by all the advice and can't believe it's really necessary to spend that much money. And it's the ultimate guide for every father looking for an excuse to get out of ante-natal classes.

Roni Jay is a professional author whose books include **KIDS & Co: winning business tactics for every family.** She is the mother of three young children, and stepmother to another three grown up ones.

Order form

You can order any of our books via any of the contact routes on page 114, including on our website. Or fill out the order form below and fax it or post it to us.

We'll normally send your copy out by first class post within 24 hours (but please allow five days for delivery). We don't charge postage and packing within the UK. Please add £1 per book for postage outside the UK.

Title (Mr/Mrs/Miss/Ms/Dr/Lord etc)

Name

Address

Postcode

Daytime phone number

Email

No. of copies	Title	Price	Total £
	Recipes for Disasters	£7.99	
	Out of Your Townie Mind	£7.99	
	Full Time Father	£9.99	
	Kids & Co	£6.99	
	Babies for Beginners	£6.99	
	The White Ladder Diaries	£9.99	
	The Voice of Tobacco	£6.99	
Postage and packing £1 per book (outside the UK only):			
		TOTAL:	

Please either send us a cheque made out to White Ladder Press Ltd or fill in the credit card details below.

Type of card ☐ Visa ☐ Mastercard ☐ Switch

Card number

Start date (if on card) _____ Expiry date _____ Issue no (Switch) _____

Name as shown on card

Signature